Élan 1
OCR

Self Study Guide

Marian Jones

OXFORD
UNIVERSITY PRESS

OXFORD
UNIVERSITY PRESS

Great Clarendon Street, Oxford OX2 6DP

Oxford University Press is a department of the University of Oxford.
It furthers the University's objective of excellence in research, scholarship,
and education by publishing worldwide in

Oxford New York

Auckland Cape Town Dar es Salaam Hong Kong Karachi
Kuala Lumpur Madrid Melbourne Mexico City Nairobi
New Delhi Shanghai Taipei Toronto

With offices in

Argentina Austria Brazil Chile Czech Republic France Greece
Guatemala Hungary Italy Japan South Korea Poland Portugal
Singapore Switzerland Thailand Turkey Ukraine Vietnam

Oxford is a registered trade mark of Oxford University Press
in the UK and in certain other countries

British Library Cataloguing in Publication Data

Data available

ISBN 978 019 915379 4

10 9 8 7 6 5 4 3 2

Typeset by Thomson

Printed in Great Britain by Ashford Colour Press Ltd.

Acknowledgements

The author and publisher would like to thank Deborah Manning (editor)
and Marie-Thérèse Bourgard (language consultant).

Contents

General Exam Tips

Here's a reminder of the topics you have studied for AS Level and which you now need to revise.

Aspects of Daily Life

▶ The family: structure and relationships; living conditions
▶ Food, drink, health, addictions
▶ Transport

Leisure and Entertainment

▶ Sport (including national sporting concerns and traditions)
▶ Tourism and related themes
▶ Leisure activities e.g. pastimes, music, films, theatre

Communication and Media

▶ Communication technology
▶ Media, e.g. written press, radio, television

Education and Training

▶ School and school life
▶ Work and training

You will be taking two examinations:

Unit 1: Speaking Test

The Speaking Test is worth 30% of your AS grade (and 15% of the full A Level).
The test lasts 15 minutes and you have 20 minutes to prepare beforehand.
You are not allowed to use a dictionary.

There are two sections:

▶ A role play
▶ Discussion of topics

Unit 2: Listening, Reading and Writing

This paper is worth 70% of your AS Level (and 35% of the full A Level) and the time allowed is two hours and 15 minutes.

There are two sections:

▶ Listening and Writing
▶ Reading and Writing

Pass grades for this examination range from A down to E. Here's an idea of what you need to be able to do.

If you pass AS Level French with an A grade, it means you can:

▶ Clearly understand spoken language, including details and people's opinions.

▶ Work out what someone is trying to say even if they don't spell it out in detail.

▶ Clearly understand written texts, understanding both the gist and the details.

▶ Talk fluently, giving your opinions and justifying them, and using a good range of vocabulary and generally accurate pronunciation.

▶ Organise your ideas and write them up well in French.

▶ Write using a wide range of vocabulary and grammatical structures without making many mistakes.

If you pass AS Level French with an E grade, it means you:

▶ Show some understanding of spoken French, even if you have difficulties when the language is complex and miss some of the details.

▶ Can sometimes work out what someone is trying to say even if they don't give all the details.

▶ Understand straightforward written texts, although you don't always understand more difficult writing.

▶ Can talk in French, and convey basic information, perhaps a little hesitantly and relying on material you have learned by heart. There is probably some English influence on your pronunciation.

▶ Can convey information in writing, perhaps with some difficulty in organising your material and expressing it.

▶ Use a range of vocabulary and structures, but quite often you make mistakes.

Preparing for the exams

You can see from these lists that when planning your revision there are really six areas you need to practise:

Speaking

Listening

Reading

Writing

Vocabulary

Grammar

There are tips on how to prepare each area overleaf.

Speaking

▶ Take every opportunity to practise speaking French – in lessons, with the language assistant, with a friend, with anyone you know who speaks French.

▶ Take an oral question from your textbook and work out a few sentences to answer it, then record them on tape and listen to see what areas still need practice – perhaps fluency, pronunciation or good use of vocabulary and structures.

▶ Don't write everything down first. You won't have a script on the day! You can write a few key words down for reference, but definitely no full sentences.

Listening

▶ Keep listening to French, ideally every day. Use a mix of extracts you have worked on and new texts.

▶ Try listening to something for which you have the transcript. Just listen first, then listen again with the transcript and, if necessary, look up unknown words. Finally, listen again without the transcript and challenge yourself to understand everything.

▶ Watching films is excellent listening practice and watching more than once is even better! Try watching with the subtitles and then without. If you find this hard going, just re-watch a short extract.

▶ French radio and TV programmes are useful, but can also be difficult. Record an extract and listen or watch it more than once. You will find it gets easier.

▶ Make sure you do some exam listening practice too!

Reading

▶ Keep reading a mix of things you read once quickly, such as a magazine, and things where you work hard at a short passage and try to understand everything. Texts from your textbook are useful for this.

▶ It's useful to note new vocabulary from your reading, but don't make it such hard work that you give up. Note, say, three new words from each text.

▶ Try a 'dual-language' reading book, where you get the original French on one page and an English translation on the opposite one. This is an excellent way to practise reading longer texts without losing heart!

▶ Search on the internet for articles in French on any topic which interests you.

Writing

▶ Practise planning essay questions. Jot down ideas for each paragraph – in French! – along with key vocabulary.

▶ Take a key paragraph from a piece of marked work, write some English prompts to remind you of its content and then write it out from memory. Concentrate especially on sections where the teacher suggested improvements.

▶ Look carefully at marked work and identify what grammar errors you are making. Then check them up in a grammar book and try some practice exercises.

▶ Make sure you are learning key vocabulary for each topic area, so that whichever subject comes up you will have some impressive words to use.

Vocabulary

▶ Learn lists of words regularly and build in time to go back over words you learned a week or two ago. Reinforcement makes them stick!

▶ Choose a system of recording new words which works for you. It could be paper lists, small sections on individual cards, recording the words and their English meanings on tape, making posters to stick on your bedroom wall ... what's important is that you are noting the words and going over them regularly!

▶ You were probably encouraged to use a good range of vocabulary in the essays you wrote during the year. Go back over them, highlighting good words and phrases and writing the English in the margin, then use this to test yourself. Words are often easier to learn in context.

Grammar

▶ Keep doing practice exercises in areas where you know you are weak.

▶ Use reading texts to practise thinking grammatically. For example, highlight a selection of adjectives, then write out the English for the phrases in which they appear. Test yourself by reproducing the French phrases accurately, complete with all the correct agreements!

▶ Keep learning from your verb tables until you know all the forms of each tense of regular verbs and the most common irregular verbs. Test yourself using a die. 1 = *je*, 2 = *tu*, 3 = *il/elle*, 4 = *nous*, 5 = *vous*, 6 = *ils/elles*. Use a verb list: choose an infinitive and a tense at random, throw the die and say the correct form of the verb. Practise until you can do it without hesitation.

The Speaking Test: what you need to know

The test has two parts: a role play and a discussion of the topics you have studied.

Role Play (5–6 minutes)
30 marks

You will be given a stimulus card in English, with information on it which you will need to convey to a French person played by the examiner.

▶ The examiner will start by introducing the situation, then you will have to ask certain questions and also answer the examiner's questions, referring to the stimulus card for the information.

▶ The last questions will ask for your opinion on some aspect of the topic. Listen carefully to what is asked and answer it fully, giving reasons for your opinion.

▶ You are allowed to make notes. Don't write out exactly what you will say, but do note some useful vocabulary.

To do well on this section you need to respond to what you are asked and give all the relevant details on each point. When asked for your opinion, make sure you give reasons and examples to justify it. Your knowledge of grammar is also important – try to use some of the vocabulary and structures you have learned during the AS course, but stick to those you feel you can use fairly accurately.

Discussion of Topics (9–10 minutes)
30 marks

You will choose one sub-topic from the list on page 4 (for example 'Leisure Activities' or 'Communication technology') and write five headings to indicate what areas you would like to discuss. The topic should be discussed in a French context, not a general one, so make sure you have facts and examples from French life. If you prefer, you can discuss a French literary text which you have read. You can use an A4 page of notes in French for reference.

This section is marked on four aspects:

▶ your knowledge of an aspect of French culture from the AS topic list and your ability to express your opinions on it.

▶ your fluency and ability to answer questions on the spot, without relying on pre-learned material.

▶ the quality of your language, in terms of good vocabulary and structures and also of accuracy.

▶ your pronunciation and intonation.

The Speaking Test: what you need to know

La situation

Vous habitez un petit village près de Street dans le Somerset. Des Français font un séjour chez vous.

La tâche

Vos amis français voudraient faire des excursions. À l'aide du dépliant vous discutez une visite à Clarks Village, un centre commercial, avec le père / la mère de la famille française (l'examinateur / l'examinatrice).

D'abord vous devez vous renseigner sur:

1 **le genre d'excursions qu'ils voudraient faire pendant leur séjour**
2 **ce qu'ils espèrent acheter comme souvenirs.**

Vous proposez une visite au centre commercial de Clarks Village. Vous devez :

▶ décrire le centre commercial et expliquer sa popularité
▶ dire le nombre et le type de magasins qu'on trouve à Clarks Village
▶ expliquer comment on peut se détendre là-bas
▶ expliquer comment on peut y aller
▶ donner les heures d'ouverture
▶ décrire ce qu'il y a à voir dans la région.

Au cours de la conversation vous discuterez aussi ...

▶ des raisons pour lesquelles ce nouveau type de centre commercial est populaire
▶ des avantages et des inconvénients de construire un tel centre dans une petite ville de 11000 habitants.

Make sure you are clear what you have to do. You start by asking the questions 1 and 2. Then you suggest a visit to Clarks Village. The examiner will ask you questions about it – make sure you give all the information possible for each one and tick off the six points on the list as you cover them.

In the preparation time, study the stimulus card carefully and find all information which is relevant to each point on the list. Think how to express it in French and how you will get round the difficulties. Simplify some expressions: 'Il y a jusqu'à 60% de réduction' conveys 'The merchandise is discounted at up to 60%'. Adapt others: you won't know the French for 'Tor', but you could call it 'un monument historique' and if you don't know 'caves', then do the best you can, perhaps by saying 'une attraction touristique qui s'appelle 'Wookey Hole Caves'. Finally, think up several arguments for each opinion question at the end.

Stimulus Card

Clarks
VILLAGE
OUTLET SHOPPING

- Clarks Village, the West Country's number one free tourist attraction, attracts 3.5 million visitors a year.
- 90 retail outlets including many well-known brands and companies.
- Merchandise discounted at up to 60%: surplus stock and quality seconds.
- Shoe Museum, King Arthur's Castle children's play area, tourist information centre and several catering venues.
- Charming village atmosphere.
- Location: Street in mid-Somerset, a short journey from Junction 23 of the M5 or from the A303. Parking for coaches and for 1,400 cars.
- Close to other West Country attractions such as Glastonbury Abbey and Tor, Wookey Hole Caves and Wells Cathedral.
- Open every day of the year except Christmas Day.
  April 1–31 October:
  9–6pm Monday to Saturday (9–5.30 in winter)
  10–5pm on Sundays.
  The village is open late every Thursday until 8pm.
- website www.clarksvillage.co.uk

The Speaking Test: what you need to know

Read and listen to one student's rehearsal for this part of the test.
Notice how she is careful to include everything which was asked
for in the six bullet points on the preparation sheet. (CD Track 1)
Remember that in the exam the examiner will interrupt you with
questions, so be prepared to respond.

Pouvez-vous décrire Clarks Village?
C'est un centre commercial, l'attraction touristique gratuite la plus
populaire du sud-ouest. Ce centre attire 3,5 millions de touristes chaque
année.

Il y a beaucoup de magasins?
Oui, il y en a environ 90. Ce sont des magasins où il y a jusqu' à 60%
de réduction sur le prix des marchandises, soit parce qu'elles datent
de la saison précédente, soit parce qu'on n'a pas vendu tout ce qu'on
a produit. Ou bien parce ce sont des marchandises de qualité un peu
inférieure. Mais il s'agit de marques très connues.

Qu'est-ce qu'on peut y faire pour se détendre?
Il y a un terrain de jeu pour les enfants, qui s'appelle King Arthur's
Castle, et un centre d'information pour les touristes. Il y a un choix
de cafés et de restaurants ainsi qu'un musée de la chaussure. En plus,
Clarks Village a le charme d'un vrai village.

C'est où exactement, ce centre?
Clarks Village se trouve au centre de la ville de Street, dans le Somerset.
C'est assez près de la sortie 23 de l'autoroute M5 et de la route nationale
A303. On peut y aller en voiture et il y a un parking pour les cars et pour
1400 voitures.

Quelles sont les heures d'ouverture?
Clarks Village est ouvert tous les jours sauf le Jour de Noël! En été, c'est-
à-dire du premier avril au 31 octobre, c'est ouvert du lundi au samedi
de 9 heures à 18 heures et le dimanche de 10 heures à 17 heures. En
hiver les heures d'ouverture sont de 9 heures à 17 heures 30 pendant la
semaine, et de 10 heures à 17 heures le dimanche. En plus, c'est ouvert
jusqu'à 20 heures tous les jeudis.

Il y a d'autres choses intéressantes à voir dans la région?
Oui, par exemple l'abbaye de Glastonbury et le Tor, qui est un
monument historique très connu. Il y a aussi les grottes de Wookey Hole
et la cathédrale de Wells.

You have to discuss the topic you choose for the second part of the oral for nine or ten minutes, so make sure you choose something you are genuinely interested in and on which you have views and opinions. Ensure too that you can find some good source material – in French! – on each aspect you want to talk about. Choose a general topic area (for instance, sport) and focus on a particular aspect (perhaps 'which sports do the French choose to play and watch?'), then break that down into five sub-headings, as shown below. You will need enough information to discuss each point for about two minutes.

A sample topic and sub-headings

L'importance du sport pour les Français

- l'importance du sport comme passe-temps en France
- les sports avec le plus grand nombre de licenciés
- la popularité des sports non-licenciés
- le foot et le rugby: les sports nationaux?
- le tour de France: une passion nationale?

The student who chose this topic got the initial idea from the opening of Unit 7 (Allez les sportifs) in her textbook. There were more facts and figures on the topic in the Teacher's Book, which she got from the French assistant. The first three bullet points were suggested in this material and she added the other two herself, by thinking about what she already knew about sport in France. She has been careful to keep each aspect in a **French** context, not a general one, and to select aspects which relate to the main theme: which sports are popular in France?

It is really important that the material you prepare for each bullet point focuses in depth on an aspect of your main theme. This student's theme is the relative popularity of different sports. For the first bullet point, she has some statistics from a survey on pastimes, showing how many people named sport as their main hobby – subdivided into playing it and watching it – and how that compared with other kinds of hobby. The second and third bullet points focus on the sports the French choose to play, and the student has statistics on the number of French people who belong to sporting organisations (2nd point) or pursue their sport individually (3rd bullet point). She knows which sports are the most popular in each category and has some opinions ready on why that might be. The 4th and 5th bullet points concentrate on spectating, rather than playing, but still relate to the main theme of popularity.

Remember, the examiner will want to know your opinions as well as facts. Why are certain sports particularly popular in France? Why do so many people like the 'non-club' activities? What do football or rugby contribute to French society? Why does the Tour de France capture the national interest? Try to predict the 'opinion questions' you could be asked and have your ideas ready!

The second part of the oral: discussing a topic

To do well on the section where you discuss a topic you have chosen, you need to show a good knowledge of the topic – with some **French** facts and figures – and also express your ideas and opinions on the topic. The examiner will guide the discussion and it is vital that you listen carefully and respond to what you are asked. Look at the opening section of a practical oral below and notice how the student gives some interesting facts and examples of French newspapers, but is also able to voice his opinion on them convincingly when asked to do so.

Chosen topic: les médias: la presse en France

Alors, vous avez fait des recherches sur des journaux français?

Oui, j'ai lu quelques exemples de journaux nationaux, comme le Monde et le Figaro où on trouve des informations internationales ainsi que françaises. Ce sont tous les deux des journaux très sérieux et intellectuels.

Et les journaux régionaux, comment sont-ils différents?

J'ai lu plusieurs journaux régionaux, comme Ouest-France et Nice-Matin, et j'ai trouvé qu'il y a quand même plusieurs pages d'articles sur la politique nationale et même étrangère, mais aussi une section importante qui traite des informations régionales.

Et quel type de journal est le plus populaire en France?

D'après les statistiques, les journaux régionaux sont beaucoup plus populaires, surtout bien sûr dans les régions. Les journaux nationaux se vendent surtout dans les grands centres comme Paris.

Et cela vous étonne, que les journaux régionaux soient si populaires?

Non. Je comprends très bien pourquoi ces journaux sont populaires dans les régions. D'abord, ils sont plus rapides à lire et plus faciles à comprendre, mais il ne manque rien. On apprend les grands thèmes nationaux du jour, mais aussi ce qui se passe dans sa région. Je pense que les journaux régionaux sont une excellente solution pour les gens pressés.

Alors, j'imagine que vous avez étudié plusieurs journaux régionaux. Pouvez-vous me citer deux exemples, et les comparer ?

Oui, par exemple .....

Notice how the examiner follows up what the candidate says. The candidate mentions national papers, so the examiner is keen to know what he knows about the very popular regional papers and follows the initial question up with one where quite lot of detailed knowledge will be required for a good answer - a description of the content of two regional papers. The next question might be one requiring a personal opinion on the papers described and then the examiner will probably move on to a different aspect, perhaps 'Quels sont les thèmes principaux qu'on trouve à la une d'un journal national français?' or 'Est-ce qu'on prend la politique internationale au sérieux dans les journaux français ?'

The second part of the oral: discussing a topic

Remember that you will also be marked for fluency and for the quality of your language. You need to talk freely, sound natural and not make too many errors! The key to this is learning – not learning a lot of sentences parrot-fashion, but rather having facts at your fingertips and being able to express them in a number of different ways so that you can react to the exact questions you are asked. Write out your key information on a side of A4 and practise expressing it in various ways. Use structures you are confident about, or check things you are unsure of with your teacher or French assistant.

You can plan your time as you wish, but there are suggested amounts of time to spend on each section

Listening and Writing (60 marks)

Suggested time: 1 hour

There will be about five minutes of recording altogether and you will be able to play it and pause it yourself. There will be three recordings to listen to, with a variety of question types:

▶ non-verbal answers such as matching activities, multiple choice questions or a gapped text with a box of words to choose from to fill the spaces

▶ comprehension questions in English

▶ a writing task based on the final listening passage, for example writing an e-mail in response to an answerphone message. There will be English prompts giving you the information you have to convey.

Reading and Writing (80 marks)

Suggested time: 1 hour 15 minutes

There will be three passages of French to read, with a variety of types of question:

▶ non-verbal answers such as multiple choice, matching or box-ticking

▶ answering short questions in French

▶ writing a longer piece in French in response to a text, summarising some of its content and then giving your own ideas or opinions.

The key ways to prepare are by:
▶ learning key vocabulary for each topic area
▶ revising the main grammar points
▶ doing plenty of listening practice to keep your ear 'tuned in' to French
▶ practising writing summary pieces and then giving your opinion on the topic
▶ working through the exam-type questions and tips on the following pages.

Écoutez cet extrait d'une interview avec une actrice. Choisissez la bonne réponse et écrivez la lettre dans la case. (CD Track 2)

(a) **Cécile vient de jouer**
   A   son premier rôle professionnel
   B   dans un film
   C   dans une pièce de théâtre

(b) **Pour elle, faire du cinéma veut dire**
   A   l'anonymat
   B   la célébrité
   C   la richesse

(c) **Si on lui demande son autographe, elle**
   A   le donne
   B   est embêtée
   C   le refuse

Listen carefully and look out for traps! For question **a**, you hear the words 'la première fois', but it would be wrong to choose answer **A**, because Cécile goes on to explain that this is her first film, but that she has also worked in theatre. For question **b**, although Cécile uses the word 'anonyme', it's not the answer because she is referring to theatre, not cinema. And for **c**, although you hear the word 'embêtée', it's not the answer because it's used negatively on the recording: 'je ne suis pas embêtée.'

When you've marked the exercise, listen again while reading the transcript.

Bonjour Cécile et bienvenue. Vous venez de tourner ce film dont tout le monde parle, mais je crois que c'est la première fois que vous faites du cinéma?

- Oui, c'est ça. J'ai déjà en plusieurs rôles au théâtre, mais ceci est mon premier film.

- Et vous trouvez que c'est très différent?

- Ah oui. Il me semble que les médias s'intéressent beaucoup plus au cinéma qu'au théâtre. J'ai fait tant d'interviews, on parle du film dans tous les journaux et on me reconnaît beaucoup plus dans la rue. Au théâtre, c'est plus anonyme, je dirais.

- Et cela vous gêne, d'être reconnue partout?

- Je pense que ça fait partie du rôle et je ne suis pas embêtée si on me parle au restaurant pour me demander mon autographe. Mais j'ai acheté un appartement très privé, donc je peux me retirer quand je veux et ça aussi, c'est important.

Écoutez le reportage, puis écrivez le mot de la liste qui convient dans chaque blanc. Mais attention, il y a cinq mots de trop! Utilisez chaque mot une fois seulement. (CD Track 3)

devenir	droit	excellent	veulent
liberté	mauvais	refusent	accepter
indépendance	bonnes	meilleur	indépendant

Théo se croit (1) _____. Ses
(2) _____ notes à l'école font confiance
à ses parents et il a un peu de liberté parce qu'il voyage souvent
le week-end avec son équipe de basket. Pour lui, la liberté
c'est le (3) _____ moyen de
(4) _____ adulte.

Juliette se plaint qu'elle n'a pas le (5) _____
de sortir en semaine et qu'elle doit rentrer assez tôt le week-
end. Ses parents ne lui permettent pas d'être indépendante et
(6) _____ de la traiter comme une adulte. Elle
voudrait plus de (7) _____.

> Use your knowledge of grammar to help you. Gaps 1 and 2 are both adjectives, but they will need different agreements. For gap 4 you need an infinitive to follow 'de'. Think too about what makes sense. Juliette tells us on the recording and also in the text that she would like more independence, so what is likely to fit into gap 7: ' She would like more …'?

agaçant.
refusent encore de me traiter comme une adulte. Je commence à trouver ça
permettre d'être plus indépendante. J'ai presque dix-huit ans et mes parents
rentrer à la maison avant minuit. Je crois que mes parents devraient me
• Non! Je n'ai pas le droit de sortir en semaine et le week-end je dois toujours
• Et toi, Juliette ?
moyen d'apprendre à devenir adulte.
basket. Cela me permet d'être indépendant. Un peu de liberté, c'est le meilleur
de questions sur mes études. Je voyage chaque week-end avec mon équipe de
• Oui, plutôt. J'ai de bonnes notes, alors mes parents ne me posent vraiment pas
Écoutez leurs réponses. D'abord Théo:
• Êtes-vous indépendant? Voici la question que nous avons posée à deux jeunes.

The Listening, Reading and Writing paper

Écoutez ces jeunes qui parlent des langues qu'ils apprennent.
Complétez les phrases en choisissant une phrase dans la
liste ci-dessous. (CD Track 4)

Vicky: J'aime bien apprendre cette langue, mais ... [____]

Adèle: Je continue avec cette langue, bien que ... [____]

Samuel: Je vais continuer mes cours, bien que ... [____]

Charles: J'ai appris cette langue pour ... [____]

Jules: Je voulais apprendre cette langue pour ... [____]

A ... pouvoir travailler dans un pays étranger.
B ... je la trouve très facile.
C ... je ne vais pas toujours à mes cours.
D ... je parle déjà bien.
E ... parler avec mes cousins.
F ... j'ai un frère qui part au Kenya.
G ... mieux profiter de mes vacances.
H ... ce soit assez difficile.

> Remember not just to listen, but also to use grammar to help you.
> Answer **F** looks as if it might be right for Charles because it mentions a
> brother going to Kenya. However, it doesn't fit grammatically because
> after 'pour', you need either a noun or a verb in the infinitive. Similarly,
> for the answers for Adèle and Samuel, whose phrases end in 'bien que',
> you need a verb in the subjunctive. Look at the three phrases which
> are (or could be!) in the subjunctive and decide which one fits with the
> meaning expressed on the recording.

Vicky: Moi, tous les lundis j'ai cours de grec, mais hier je n'y suis pas allée! J'ai
complètement oublié!

Adèle: J'adore les langues et je parle assez bien l'allemand et l'anglais, mais j'ai eu
des difficultés avec le japonais. C'est une langue très compliquée, je trouve.

Samuel: J'ai une excellente prof d'italien et j'ai déjà fait des progrès. Mais je
continue les cours, parce que je voudrais le parler encore mieux.

Charles: Mon frère part au Kenya, où il va enseigner dans une école primaire. Moi
aussi, j'ai fait un tel stage et donc quand il essaie d'apprendre le swahili, je peux
l'aider.

Jules: Je suis invité au Maroc pour tout ce mois cet été. Je suis en train
d'apprendre quelques mots d'arabe avant de partir.

dix-sept 17

Listen carefully to this report on mobile phones and provide the information required in English. (CD Track 5)

a Why do young children like to have their own mobile phones? (*2 marks*)

_____

_____

b Why might parents be against this? (*2 marks*)

_____

_____

c What advantages might there be if parents agree to children having a mobile? (*4 marks*)

_____

_____

Use the marks allocated per question as a guide to make sure you give **all** the **relevant** detail. Questions a and b have two obvious answers each. Question c also has two main answers, but the second one has extra detail which you will need to convey in order to get all four marks. Remember too that you need to give the exact answers from the text and not be tempted to write your own ideas on any of these matters!

Trop jeune pour un portable?

Même les moins de dix ans veulent tous leur propre portable, surtout pour „faire grand‟ et pour rester en contact avec leurs amis à toute heure. Mais, pas tous les parents sont d'accord, soit parce qu'ils craignent les risques pour la santé, soit tout simplement parce qu'un portable est une dépense supplémentaire et ils ont peur que leurs enfants en perdent plusieurs avant l'âge de responsabilité. Mais n'oublions pas les avantages: si on laisse son enfant sortir seul, peut-être pour se rendre chez un copain, on sait qu'il ou elle peut toujours téléphoner en cas de difficulté. Et un enfant qui a un portable se sert beaucoup moins du téléphone de maison – un plus, si on veut téléphoner soi-même ou si on attend un appel important!

The Listening, Reading and Writing paper

This writing question is based on the listening extract for the previous exercise. If you have time, listen to it once more while thinking about the writing question and note down any useful ideas or vocabulary.

Here's an example question.

Write to the radio programme which broadcast the piece on children and mobile phones. Write in French in continuous prose and include all the points your friend made in his English piece. You do not have to translate the piece word for word.

I found the programme on mobile phones interesting (1) and I agree that mobile phones are rather expensive for children (1). There is always a danger that they might lose the phone (1) or that another child will try to steal it (1). There are health risks too, especially for very young children (1).

But mobile phones are useful (1) if children are out without their parents (1) They therefore allow children a degree of independence (1) and parents can contact their children at any time (1).

However I don't think every young child needs a mobile of their own (1).

Obvious as it sounds, you must convey all the information in the English piece in order to get all ten marks for communication! To help you with this, the numbers in brackets highlight the ten points for which communication marks would be given, but remember that the examination piece will **not** be annotated like this. It will be up to you to make sure you include everything!

Remember that your task is to get the information across, not necessarily to translate it word for word. So if there are some difficult phrases, try to think of ways to simplify them.

There are also ten marks for the quality of your language. Try to stick to expressions which sound 'French' rather than 'translated from English'. Be careful over accuracy, keeping to French you can handle well and giving verb endings, adjective agreements and spellings a thorough last check.

Qui pense quoi? Lisez les textes et cochez sept cases dans la grille.

	Saïda	Thibaut	Jean	Camille
1 Il / Elle trouve que c'est bon de rester chez soi pour les vacances.				
2 Il /Elle aime partir et voir ailleurs.				
3 Le tourisme est bon pour l'économie.				
4 Les vacances coûtent trop cher.				
5 Le tourisme est mauvais pour l'environnement.				

Saïda
Je ne vois pas pourquoi on est contre le tourisme pour des raisons "éthiques". Les touristes dépensent leur argent dans nos magasins et ils soutiennent toutes sortes d'autres entreprises, comme les hôtels, les restaurants, ou les centres sportifs.

Thibaut
Si tout le monde voyageait n'importe quand, que nous resterait-il de la terre qu'on pense tant aimer? Je peux très bien faire des excursions entre amis et près de chez moi et je n'ai pas besoin de gaspiller nos ressources de pétrole pour me rendre ailleurs.

Jean
Rester chez moi toute l'année? Ce n'est pas si mal et je suis fier de dire que je ne prends pas l'avion deux ou trois fois par an pour me détendre. C'est une question de responsabilité.

Camille
Je trouve qu'il est intéressant d'aller voir la vie dans d'autres régions et d'autres pays, et pour moi les voyages sont un plaisir et une expérience à ne pas manquer. Cependant je comprends aussi les arguments écologiques contre les voyages pas "nécessaires".

Read any sentence – in the text or in the statements – which has a negative in it very carefully. It might look as if Saïda is against tourism for ethical reasons if you don't take note of the beginning of her sentence: 'je ne vois pas pourquoi ...' You could think that Jean doesn't want to spend all year at home until you read the next sentence: 'ce n'est pas si mal'. Camille uses a negative phrase to underline how much she enjoys holidays: 'une experience à ne pas manquer'.

The Listening, Reading and Writing paper

Lisez le texte, puis répondez aux questions en français.

De récentes études ont montré que la consommation de boissons gazeuses (surtout les colas) peut provoquer un risque accru de fracture, surtout chez les jeunes dont les os sont encore en train de se développer. On soupçonne les phosphates présents dans ce type de boisson d'être responsables d'une fragilisation des os, en nuisant à l'absorption ou à l'utilisation du calcium. Plusieurs facteurs sont à considérer dans cette association:

▶ la caféine dans les colas favorise la perte de calcium dans l'urine.

▶ la surconsommation de boissons gazeuses mène souvent à une consommation moins forte de lait, une excellente source de calcium.

▶ les mauvaises habitudes alimentaires sont souvent accompagnées par un manque d'activité physique, ce qui peut aussi nuire aux os.

Thème peu important? Il faut noter que la moitié des Canadiens de 11 à 15 ans consomment tous les jours des boissons gazeuses.

a Que font les jeunes qui leur donne un plus grand risque de fracture des os? ....

....

b Quel effet nuisible ont les phosphates dans ces boissons?

....

c Nommez deux habitudes typiques chez ceux qui consomment beaucoup de boissons gazeuses qui sont eux aussi nuisibles à la santé. ....

....

This type of question usually requires you to manipulate the language of the text. The easiest way to answer question **a** is to take the noun 'la consommation' and turn it into a verb: 'ils consomment …' . Question **b** can be answered by taking 'favorise' from the text and making it plural to follow 'ils …'. The phrases 'une consommation moins forte de lait' and 'un manque d'activité physique' give you the answers for question **c**, but you will have to manipulate them. Think of a verb for each (perhaps 'consommer' or 'boire' and 'faire') and start your answer with 'Ils…'. It's useful to collect vocabulary in 'families' – verbs, adjectives, nouns with the same root – to help you manipulate the language of a text.

Remember that there are ten extra marks for Quality of Language on this question, so check your answers carefully for accuracy.

Lisez l'article, puis répondez aux questions.

La pub: pour ou contre?

On se plaint souvent de la quantité de publicité qu'on trouve dans les médias. J'en ai parlé avec trois étudiants de l'université de Nantes. Lisez mon interview, puis formez-vous une opinion!

Alors, Benoît, trouvez-vous qu'il y a trop de publicité de nos jours?

Ça dépend naturellement de son point de vue. Des fois, au cinéma, je vois une annonce pour un film dont je ne sais pas grand-chose et qui a l'air intéressant et je décide d'aller le voir. C'est avantageux, quand même. D'un autre côté, quand il s'agit sans pause de bonbons et de glaces, j'enrage.

Et pour vous, Faustine. La publicité vous intéresse?

Ben, je trouve que c'est très facile d'être contre toute publicité, mais je dois avouer que j'y trouve un certain intérêt. Il y a certaines pubs qui sont des œuvres artistiques, avec leur sens de l'humour et l'attention qu'on prête à chaque petit détail – le slogan, la musique, les couleurs.

Louis, vous êtes d'accord?

Moi, je réussis à éviter la publicité! Je n'ai pas beaucoup de patience avec la télévision, parce que je trouve que c'est barbant quand on regarde une émission qu'on aime, d'avoir toujours ces interminables publicités. Je n'ai jamais vu une publicité que j'ai trouvée intéressante.

(a) **Basez vos réponses sur le texte.**

Quels sont les avantages et les inconvénients de la publicité selon les trois étudiants?

(b) **Et vous? Êtes-vous pour ou contre la publicité? Justifiez votre opinion.**

The Listening, Reading and Writing paper

Question (a) asks you to pick through the text selecting particular information: in this case points for and against advertising. Similarly, you could be asked for the causes and effects of a problem or to select facts and opinions on a topic. You need to read the whole text through, underlining the relevant sections, perhaps in two different colours to keep them separate in your mind, and then to write them up without copying the original. If you work systematically through a task like this, you should do it well.

You need to be organised. The key words are PLAN – WRITE – CHECK.

PLAN question (a) by highlighting the text, as described above.

PLAN question (b) by jotting down any ideas which come to mind, then selecting a range of good ones and putting them in a logical order. Re-read your plan, noting useful words or expressions you would like to include.

WRITE the piece up carefully, referring to your PLAN and don't be tempted to deviate from your notes. Think grammatically as you form the sentences, and think in French. It doesn't work well to decide what you want to say in English, then try and force that into French!

Allow time to CHECK your writing. Does every sentence make sense? Do the verbs agree with their subject? Are all the adjective agreements in place? Look twice at the spelling of tricky words. Check for missing accents.

The marks for this question break down as follows:

Comprehension of the text – 15 marks. You need to include all the relevant points to get maximum marks for question (a).

Response to the text – 20 marks. To do well you must express opinions well, backing them up with reasons, and you should show some originality and imagination.

Accuracy of language – 10 marks. For this you must show that you can handle tenses and agreements well and use complex language without making many errors.

Range of language – 10 marks. The key here is variety. Choose interesting words and structures, including some of the more complex structures you have learned at AS Level. But choose only those you can use accurately!

> Remember that there is grammar practice on the grammar points listed below for you to work through on the CD which comes with this book. There is more practice in the *Élan* Student's Book and in the *Élan* Grammar Workbook.

1 Nouns

1.1 Gender and plurals of nouns

Some nouns have the gender you expect (*acteur/actrice*) and there are 'typical' masculine and feminine endings which make it easier to guess the gender of a noun.

Form most plurals by adding an -*s*, but beware of exceptions such as words ending in -*s*, -*x* or -*z*, which usually stay the same and other typical exceptions such as *animal/animaux* and *jeu/jeux*.

(1) **Give the gender of:** *alcoolisme, obésité, niveau, tolérance, mariage, certitude.*
Give the plural of: *journal, portable, prix, émission, conflit.*

1.2 *de* + noun

This construction translates 'some'.

de + *le* → *du*   *de* + *la* → *de la*
de + *l'* → *de l'*   *de* + *les* → *des*

1.3 *ce*

Ce means 'this' and changes according to number and gender: ***ce** garçon,* ***cet*** *événement,* ***cette*** *difficulté,* ***ces*** *problèmes.*

1.4 *tout*

Tout means 'all' and changes according to number and gender: ***tout*** *le temps,* ***toute*** *la classe,* ***tous*** *les films,* ***toutes*** *les pièces.*

(2) **Translate into French: this job, those candidates, some effort, some tourism, all the ideas.**

2 Adjectives

2.1 Masculine, feminine and plural adjectives

Adjectives agree in number and gender with the noun they describe: *un bon moment, de bons moments.*
Most adjectives add an -*e* for the feminine version, but there are common exceptions: *premier/première, heureux/heureuse, créatif/créative, public/publique.* Most add an -*s* for the plural, but exceptions include *normal/normaux* and *beau/beaux.*

Irregular adjectives include *beau, nouveau, long, fou, frais* and *vieux*. Adjectives usually go after the noun they describe, but certain adjectives go before it; examples include *grand, petit, bon, mauvais, joli, gros* and *excellent*.

(3) Translate into French: an interesting programme, some good ideas, a fascinating book, bad publicity, an ambitious young actress.

2.2 Possessive adjectives

	m.	**f.**	**plural**
my	*mon*	*ma*	*mes*
your	*ton*	*ta*	*tes*
his/her	*son*	*sa*	*ses*
our	*notre*	*notre*	*nos*
your	*votre*	*votre*	*vos*
their	*leur*	*leur*	*leurs*

(4) Give the right possessive adjective: (my) *sport préféré*, (his) *baskets*, (our) *équipe*, (your) *but*, (their) *victoire*.

3 Adverbs

Adverbs are used to say how something is done: easily, quietly, etc.
To form an adverb in French, you usually add *-ment* to the feminine form of the adjective.
normal ⟶ *normale* ⟶ ***normalement*** = normally
heureux ⟶ *heureuse* ⟶ ***heureusement*** = happily
Exceptions include adjectives ending in *-ent* or *-ant* which follow the pattern *constant/**constamment*** and those which change the final *-e* to *-é* such as *précis/**précisément*** and *énorme/**énormément***.
Irregulars include *très, assez, trop, beaucoup* and *bien*.

4 Comparisons

Use *plus, moins* or *aussi* to compare two things.
*Julien est **plus sportif** que Florence.*
*Elle est **moins intelligente** que lui.*
*Mais elle est **aussi intelligente** que ses frères.*
The exceptions are *bon/meilleur* (better) and *mauvais/pire* (worse).

Use *le plus* or *le moins* to form a superlative.
*C'est la destination de vacances **la plus populaire** chez les Français.*
Le meilleur (the best) and *le pire* (the worst) are exceptions.
*C'est elle qui fait **la meilleure** cuisine.*

(5) Translate into French: she understands easily; he is the best footballer; does she normally speak so fast? are boys sportier than girls?

5 Prepositions

Use *à* to talk about time (*à trois heures*), distance (*à trois kilomètres d'ici*) and in phrases like *à Noël, à vélo* and *à pied*.

Use *de* to mean 'from' (*une lettre de sa mère*), to denote possession (*la voiture de mon frère*) and in phrases like *les vacances de Noël*.

Use *en* to talk about going to or being in feminine countries (*en France, en Italie*), to refer to time (*en juin, en 2012*) and in phrases like *en bateau, en anglais, en coton* and *en bonne santé*. Notice the difference between 'en une heure' (i.e. it takes that long) and 'dans une heure' (in an hour from now).

Some prepositions refer to position: *devant, derrière, sous, sur, entre*.

Other prepositions include *après, avant, avec, chez, depuis, par, pendant, pour, sans, vers*.

(6) Give the correct preposition for each phrase: *Tu habites ... quelle distance de Nantes? Les vêtements sont-ils ... bonne condition? Il travaille à la banque ... deux ans. Vous lui avez parlé ... son avenir? J'ai passé la soirée ... Marion.*

6 Pronouns

6.1 Subject, direct and indirect object pronouns

Subject	Direct object	Indirect object
je	me	me
tu	te	te
il	le	lui
elle	la	lui
nous	nous	nous
vous	vous	vous
ils	les	leur
elles	les	leur

Use subject pronouns to replace a noun which is the subject of the verb.
Je ne comprends pas.
Use direct object pronouns if the noun replaced is the object of the verb.
*Je ne **te** comprends pas.*
Use indirect object pronouns to convey the idea of English prepositions such as 'to' or 'for'.
*Tu **lui** as donné le cadeau?*
Did you give the present to him?

6.2 Emphatic pronouns

The emphatic pronouns are *moi, toi, lui, elle, nous, vous, eux, elles.*
They are used for a number of reasons, including emphasis (*Moi, je ne te crois pas*), after prepositions (*Tu y vas avec eux?*), after *c'est* and *ce sont* (*Ce sont elles qui n'ont plus d'argent!*), as a one word answer to a question (*Qui? Lui?*) and in comparisons (*Tu es plus riche que nous!*)

6.3 Reflexive pronouns

The reflexive pronouns *me, te, se, nous, vous, se* are used to form reflexive verbs: *je me lève, elle se dépêche, nous nous brossons les dents, ils se contentent de ...*

7 Translate into French: Do you see it? Will she write to him? Are they going without us? We are not enjoying ourselves.

8 Make up four sentences, each using one of these pronouns: *il, le, lui, se.*

6.4 *y* and *en*

The pronoun *y* replaces the preposition *à*, used either with a noun (*Tu vas au parc? Oui, j'y vais.*) or with a verb (*Tu penses à ton voyage? Oui, j'y pense tout le temps.*).

The pronoun *en* replaces *du, de la* or *des* after a noun (*Vous avez du papier? Oui, j'en ai.*) or it replaces *de* in a verbal construction such as *discuter de:* (*Notez vos idées. Nous en discuterons.*).

6.5 Position of pronouns

Object pronouns come before the verb, or in a compound tense, before the part of *avoir* or *être.*
Je les aime.
Je ne les ai pas vus.
If there are two verbs, the object pronoun comes before the infinitive.
Je vais en prendre un.
Vous ne pouvez pas y aller!

When there are several object pronouns in the same sentence, they come in this order:

me				
te	le	lui		
se	la	leur	y	en
nous	les			
vous				

Examples
Tu le lui a déjà donné?
Vous pouvez me l'envoyer demain?
Des bonbons? Il n'y en a plus!

(9) Translate into French: She rings us every night. They write to him every week. I have already told him that. We will give it to you. Can you repeat it for me?

6.6 Relative pronouns

qui	who, which, that
que	who, which, that
où	where, when
dont	whose, of whom, of which (recognition only)

Use *qui* when the noun to be replaced is the subject of the verb.
*J'ai un frère **qui** s'appelle Ahmed.*

Use *que* when the noun to be replaced is the object of the verb.
*J'ai un frère **que** j'aime beaucoup.*

Use *où* to mean 'where' or 'when'.
*C'est là **où** j'habite.*
*C'était le jour **où** je suis arrivé.*

Use *dont* to mean 'of whom' or 'whose'.
*C'est le prof **dont** je t'ai parlé.*
*Le directeur, **dont** le bureau est au fond du couloir, n'est jamais là.*

(10) Which relative pronoun is needed for each gap? *C'est celui ... la femme est directrice? C'est le stylo ... tu cherches? Avec ... allez·vous en vacances? C'est un film ... j'ai beaucoup apprécié. Je lui ai montré le bureau ... je travaille.*

6.7 Possessive pronouns (recognition only)

	m.	f.	m. plural	f. plural
mine	*le mien*	*la mienne*	*les miens*	*les miennes*
yours	*le tien*	*la tienne*	*les tiens*	*les tiennes*
his/hers	*le sien*	*la sienne*	*les siens*	*les siennes*
ours	*le nôtre*	*la nôtre*	*les nôtres*	*les nôtres*
yours	*le vôtre*	*la vôtre*	*les vôtres*	*les vôtres*
theirs	*le leur*	*la leur*	*les leurs*	*les leurs*

*J'aime bien tes parents. **Les miens** m'énervent.*
*Je ne m'entends pas bien avec ma sœur, mais je m'entends bien avec **la tienne**.*

6.8 Demonstrative pronouns

Use these to say 'the one(s) which'.

	singular	**plural**
masculine	*celui*	*ceux*
feminine	*celle*	*celles*

J'aime bien mon pull, mais je préfère **celui** *de Paul.*
Je m'occupe des jeunes enfants, **ceux** *qui ont moins de cinq ans.*

(11) **Decide on the correct possessive pronoun or demonstrative pronoun for each gap:** *Quelle robe préfères-tu? ... avec la ceinture? Il aime bien mon ordinateur, mais il a des difficultés avec ...* (**his**)*. Vos idées ne sont pas mauvaises, mais ...* (**ours**) *sont meilleures! Lequel des deux? ... aux cheveux blonds?*

7 Verbs

7.1 The infinitive

The infinitive is the unconjugated form of the verb: *parler* – to speak, *devoi*r – to have to, *vendre* – to sell.
Infinitives are used in several ways:

- as nouns: ***travailler****, quelle horreur!*
- in instructions: ***mettre** à four chaud.*
- as the second verb in a clause: *on doit **passer** un examen; je vais **voir** le dentiste tous les six mois; il faut **faire** un effort.*
- after the prepositions *à* and *de*: *il se met à **pleuvoir** ; qu'est-ce que tu as décidé de **faire***?
- after *pour, sans* and *avant de*: *on ne peut pas progresser sans connaître la grammaire; prenez votre temps avant de **répondre**.*

The past infinitive is used to say 'after having done' something and is based on the perfect tense using *avoir* or *être*.
*Après **avoir mangé**, il est parti.*
*Après **être rentrées**, mes sœurs ont bu un café.*

(12) **Translate into French:** He hates revising. After having finished, I left. Do you want to leave now? After having arrived, they phoned us.

7.2 The present tense

Use the present tense to say what someone does or is doing. It can also be used to describe events in the very near future.

Grammar Summary

Regular verbs

-er verbs: *aimer: j'aime, tu aimes, il/elle aime, nous aimons, vous aimez, ils/elles aiment*

-ir verbs: *choisir: je choisis, tu choisis, il/elle choisit, nous choisissons, vous choisissez, ils/elles choisissent*

-re verbs: *vendre: je vends, tu vends, il/elle vend, nous vendons, vous vendez, ils vendent*

Irregular verbs: learn these by heart.

(13) **Translate into French: Are you coming?** *(tu)* **They take. We go. He finishes. They (fem.) are waiting. I can. She sees. You write** *(vous).*

7.3 The perfect tense

Use the perfect tense to describe completed actions which happened in the past. Use it in conversations, letters and informal narratives.

The perfect tense is made up of two parts: the auxiliary verb (part of *avoir* or *être*) and the past participle.
Past participles of regular verbs follow this pattern:

-er verbs : *aimer: aimé*

-ir verbs : *choisir: choisi*

-re verbs : *vendre: vendu*

Learn the past participles of the main irregular verbs – see the verb table again.

Example verbs which take *avoir: j'ai fini, ils ont acheté, vous avez mis, nous avons fait.*

The main verbs which take *être* are *arriver/partir, entrer/sortir, aller/venir, monter/descendre, tomber/rester* and *naître/mourir.* Verbs derived from these 12 also take *être*, e.g. *rentrer, revenir, devenir.* All reflexive verbs also take *être.*

Remember that agreement is needed on the past participles of verbs which take *être.* Add -e (feminine), -s (plural) or -es (feminine plural).

Example verbs which take *être: je suis allé* (masculine), *nous sommes devenues* (feminine plural), *ils se sont levés* (masculine plural), *tu es parti?* (masculine).

One last thing to remember: if a verb which takes *avoir* is used with a direct object which comes before the verb, then agreement with the direct object – not the subject –will be needed:
Où est la veste que Marc a achetée? Je ne l'ai pas vue.

(14) **Write these verbs out in the perfect tense:**
je/faire, ils/prendre, nous/aller, elle/se laver, tu/mettre, il/parler, vous/rentrer, elles/boire

7.4 The imperfect tense

The imperfect tense is used to describe what things were like, to say what was happening, to describe things which happened frequently or, after *si*, to suggest doing something.

> *J'allais tous les jours à la plage.*
> *Il regardait la télévision quand le téléphone a sonné.*
> *Si on dansait?*

Form the imperfect using the *nous* form of the present tense (minus the *-ons*), with the endings *-ais, -ais, -ait, -ions, -iez, -aient*.
regarder → *nous regardons* → *je regardais*
faire → *nous faisons* → *vous faisiez*
The only exception is *être*: *j'étais, tu étais*, etc.

15 **Give the imperfect form for these verbs:**
 je/lire tu/finir elle/boire nous/travailler vous/aller ils/faire

7.5 The pluperfect tense

Use the pluperfect to say what **had** happened.
Form it using the auxiliary verbs *avoir* and *être* in the imperfect:
Le prof m'a dit qu'il m'avait donné une bonne note.
Je suis arrivé trop tard et mes copains étaient déjà partis.

16 **Think of an ending in the pluperfect tense for each sentence:**
 J'ai fait une erreur parce que … Ils n'ont pas réussi aux examens parce qu'ils … Nous étions en retard parce que …

7.6 The future tense

You can use the present tense to refer to something fairly certain in the near future.
Je vais à l'université de Leeds l'année prochaine.
To talk about something which is sure to happen in the near future you can use *je vais* + infinitive:
Je vais regarder le film ce soir.
To talk about future plans which are not certain, use *je voudrais …*, *j'aimerais …*, or *je pense …* plus an infinitive:
Je pense rentrer dans l'armée de l'air.
Je voudrais faire le tour du monde.

Use the future tense to describe other less certain or more distant events, or in *si* clauses.
Quand il sera à la retraite, il ira habiter en France.
Si j'ai mon bac, j'irai à l'université.
Remember you also need the future tense to describe 'what will happen when …', unlike English where the present tense is used.
Quand ils arriveront, on parlera de tout ça.
Dites-lui de me contacter dès qu'il aura ses résultats.

Grammar Summary

To form the future of regular verbs, use the infinitive (minus the -e on -re verbs) and the endings -ai, -as, -a, -ons, -ez, -ont: *je regarderai, tu attendras, ils ne partiront pas.*

Learn the future stem of irregular verbs, then add the same endings: *je ferai, elle viendra, vous serez.*

(17) **Give the future form of each verb:** *je/devoir tu/vendre il/se lever nous/savoir vous/voir ils/choisir*

7.7 The future perfect tense

This is used to explain what **will have happened**.
It is made up of *avoir* or *être* in the future tense and a past participle.
*Je **serai partie** quand il arrivera.*

(18) **Translate into French: What are you doing tonight? Are you thinking of going to the theatre? Will you go on holiday again? When you are twenty, you will be at university. Will you have received the letter?**

7.8 The conditional tense

This is used to explain what **would** happen.
It is formed using the future stem of the verb (regular or irregular) and the endings
-ais, -ais, -ait, -ions, -iez, -aient.
*Elle **devrait** faire des études à l'étranger.*
*Si j'avais une voiture, **j'irais** chercher les enfants.*

(19) **Write out what each person would do if they won the lottery:** *je, tu, il, nous, vous, ils.*

7.9 The imperative

This is used to give orders, instructions or advice.
To form it, leave out the subject pronouns *tu* or *vous* (and leave the final -s off the *tu* form of -er verbs).
Va voir!
Viens ici!
Essayez de lui parler.

The few irregulars include *avoir* (*aie, ayez*), *être* (*sois, soyez*) and *savoir* (*sache, sachez*).
For negative imperatives, use *ne* and *pas*: *ne fais pas ça!*

(20) **Write out three requests to a small child you are looking after and three more to your boss at work.**

7.10 The subjunctive

Use the subjunctive:

- after verbs expressing doubt: *je ne pense pas que ...*
- after verbs expressing an emotion or desire: *je suis contente que, je voudrais que ...*
- after impersonal verbs such as *il faut que ...*
- after certain conjunctions including *avant que, bien que, afin que, pour que, à condition que ...*
- after a relative pronoun when it follows a superlative or negative: *c'est la plus jolie region que je connaisse; je n'ai rien qui puisse t'aider.*

To form the present subjunctive, take the *ils* form of the present tense, leave off the final ·*ent* and add the endings -*e, -es, -e, -ions, -iez, -ent.* Learn the common irregular forms such as *j'aille (aller), j'aie (avoir), je sois (être) je fasse (faire)* and *je puisse (pouvoir).*

21 **Write a suitable verb in the subjunctive in each gap.** *Je ne suis pas sûr que ce ... réaliste. Elle voudrait que je ... à l'heure. Pour arriver ce soir, il faut que vous ... tout de suite.*

8 The passive

A sentence is in the passive when its subject has the action done to it instead of doing it.
To form the passive use *être* and a past participle agreeing with the subject of the verb: *les enfants en difficulté sont aidés par notre association.*
The passive can be used in other tenses: *seront aidés, ont été aidés, étaient aidés, avaient été aidés.*

22 **Translate into French: This will be done. That wasn't finished. The letter hasn't been written.**

9 The negative

To make a verb negative, use *ne* and *pas*: *Ce n'est pas vrai.*
Before an infinitive, use *ne* and *pas* together: *je préfère ne pas y aller.*
Other negative constructions include *ne ... jamais, ne ... plus, ne ... personne, ne ... que* and *ne ... rien.*
Il ne faut jamais faire cela.
Je n'ai rien fait.

When you use a negative with a noun, remember to use *de*: *tu n'as plus de chocolat?*

23 **Write five negative sentences about the media, using a different negative in each one.**

Pronunciation

Listening to plenty of French helps improve your pronunciation. So will working through specific exercises like the ones below. It can be tricky to correct bad habits, so if a teacher or assistant gives you advice on the way you pronounce a particular sound, make a written note of it and refer back to it occasionally to make sure you really have remembered it.

1 Les voyelles: a, è, é, i, o, u

Écoutez et répétez le son de six voyelles françaises.

a	habite, déjà, femme	a à e + mm
è	frère, fête, treize, aide, aîné vaisselle, ancienne princesse, baguette	è ê ei ai aî e + ll, e + nn, e + ss, e + tt
é	télévision, lycée, aller, pied, chez, mes effet, essayer	é ée er ed ez es e + ff, e + ss
i	ici, dîner, lycée, égoïste, prix, nuit	i î y ix it ï
o	chose, faux, beaucoup, bientôt	o au eau ô
u	musique sûr	u û

2 Les sons 'é', 'ais', 'è', 'ère', 'er'

Écoutez et répétez ces différents sons français.

e – liberté, réussir, métier, école, indépendant
ai, ais – faire, aide, maison, parfait, vraiment
è – bibliothèque, système, succède, être, crêpes
ère – chère, père, mère, frère, colère
er – aller, donner, changer, essayer, expliquer

3 Les sons 'in', 'an', 'on', 'un', 'en'

Écoutez et répétez ces différents sons français.

in – intéressant, international, matin, important, impossible, pain, plein, peinture
an – vacances, océan, restaurant, pendant, blanc, chambre
on – rencontrer, dont, combien, nombreux, complet
un – un, chacun, brun, opportun
en – moment, enrichissant, alimentation, empêcher, temps

4 Les liaisons

Lisez ces phrases à haute voix en faisant attention aux liaisons. Écoutez pour vérifier.

1 De nombreux accidents de la route sont tout à fait évitables.
2 Il y a un écart de huit ans entre l'espérance de vie des hommes et des femmes.

3 À trois heures dix, six voitures entraient en collision sur l'autoroute du soleil.

4 À Paris, il y a parfois quatre ou cinq pharmacies les unes après les autres.

5 L'intonation: questions et exclamations

L'intonation: la voix monte ou descend. Écoutez et répétez.

1 Les questions simples: Tu vas au lycée? Aimez-vous votre lycée?
Les questions avec un interrogatif: À quel âge es-tu allé au lycée?
Que pensez-vous du lycée?
Les questions – énumération: Tu es pour ou contre? Tu envisages des études longues, des études courtes ou la vie active?
Les exclamations: Alors là, catastrophe! Moi, j'adore mon lycée!

Lisez tout haut, puis écoutez pour vérifier et répétez.

2 En quelle année es-tu entré en sixième? Tu es allé dans un lycée après?
Tu préfères les maths ou le français? Moi, je vais y arriver! Tu fais anglais, allemand ou italien? Je déteste ça!

6 Le 'r' français

En français, il faut rouler le 'r' un peu dans la gorge. Écoutez et répétez.

1 rouge, rhythme, rollers, repas, relax, racontez
2 arrêtez! Je suis arrivé.
3 c'est fermé, moderne, le chef du personnel
4 j'ai travaillé, j'ai préparé, j'ai créé
5 Robert m'a raconté qu'elle avait regardé les répétitions.
6 Valérie rentre en France au printemps.

7 Les consonnes que l'on ne prononce pas

En général, les consonnes s, t, d, p, x placées à la fin d'un mot ne se prononcent pas. Écoutez et lisez, puis répétez.

1 s – accès excès Paris   s – les médias préférées des jeunes
   t – le débat, le droit de tout savoir   d, x – Le Canard Enchaîné, La Voix
                                                     du Nord
   p – Il y a beaucoup trop de publicité à la télé.

Cependant, des consonnes se prononcent lorsqu'elles sont suivies d'un 'e'. Écoutez et lisez, puis répétez.

2 les Français   la radio française   il est mort elle est morte
   il fait chaud   des températures chaudes

8 'o' ouvert – o fermé – ou

Écoutez et répétez les trois sons:

1 'o' ouvert – solaire, bénévole, solution
   'o' fermé – beau, frigo, eau
   'ou' – souvent, trouver, groupe

Pronunciation

Classez ces mots en trois listes selon le son souligné, puis vérifiez en écoutant.

s<u>au</u>vage n<u>o</u>cif pel<u>ou</u>se d<u>ou</u>che ois<u>eau</u> t<u>o</u>xique les V<u>o</u>sges n<u>ou</u>velle bl<u>oc</u>-notes se<u>au</u> p<u>o</u>litique ren<u>ou</u>velable

2 'o' ouvert – nocif, toxique, bloc-notes, politique
  'o' fermé – sauvage, oiseau, les Vosges, seau
  'ou' – pelouse, douche, nouvelle, renouvelable

Lisez les phrases à haute voix. Écoutez pour vérifier et répétez.

3 Tu es populaire avec tes co-équipiers? Il nous faut une nouvelle politique sur la technologie. L'opération de communication a été un grand succès. Les bénévoles espèrent sauver les oiseaux des produits toxiques.

9 Prononciation de 'in' et 'im'

in-/im- + consonne sauf n et m   im-/im- + voyelle, n, m

Écoutez et répétez.

intégration, interview, imbécile, important
inadmissible, innocent, image, immigré

10 L'accent du mot

L'accent principal du mot français tombe sur la dernière syllabe. Lisez les phrases. Écoutez pour vérifier et répétez.

C'est inexact de dire que l'immigration implique l'insécurité. L'inegalité des chances et l'injustice sont indéniables. Il est acceptable et inexcusable qu'un pays industrialisé soit incapable d'intégrer des immigrés.

11 Les sons 'ille', 'gn'

Écoutez et répétez.

1 ville, tranquille, mille, million, millier
2 fille, famille, billet, gentille, habillement
3 travailler, bouteille, accueille, ailleurs, j'aille, je veuille, grenouille, rataouille
4 Allemagne, Espagne, Bretagne, Avignon, signer, ignore, oignon, enseignement
5 Des milliers de filles vivent à Avignon.
  On mange une bouillabaisse ou des cuisses de grenouille? Moi, je préfère de l'agneau avec une sauce à l'oignon. Des gentilles filles de la ville de Marseille font la ratatouille et la bouillabaisse à merveille.

12 Trois voyelles: 'a', 'u', 'o'

Écoutez et répétez.

1 Louisiane, Guyane, platane, banane
2 une, lune, dune, prune
3 couverture, voiture, écriture
4 francophone, anglophone, téléphone

It's always a good idea to do something with the words you are trying to learn, rather than just looking at them. Here are some ideas to try out.

▶ Group the words you are learning, for example by writing lists of synonyms or opposites.

la victoire / la défaite, perdre / gagner, en forme / malsain, sédentaire / actif ...

▶ List words in 'families'. If you have noted the verb, can you find a noun or an adjective which is related to it?

comprendre	*la compréhension*	*compréhensif*
exiger	*l'exigence*	*exigeant*
mentir	*le menteur/la mensonge*	*menteur*

▶ Write out a set of words in jumbled form, then come back a few days later and try to unjumble them. Can you sort out these eight words on the topic of smoking and drinking?

m r u f e	*g s t b a i e a m*	*l l o o h c*
s s r v e e i	*e i i s u l b n*	*p l o o c p a*
o o m u n p s	*c c n r e a*	

(fumer, tabagisme, alcool, ivresse, nuisible, alcoopo, poumons, cancer)

▶ Write out words with gaps for missing letters or sentences with key words gapped and then try to fill them in later. Complete these words which are all linked to newspapers.

he-doma-aire	*-en-uel*	*pu-lici-é,*
qu-ti-ien	*le-teur*	*re-orta-e*

▶ Choose, say, three words from a particular topic area and challenge yourself to say or write a sentence including them all. Try the following:

le divorce — le partenaire — monoparental
équilibré — poids — la forme
le métier — le chômage — la rémunération

▶ Fill as many words from one topic as you can into a word square, then solve it a week later when you have forgotten where you put them.

Expressions-clés

Time phrases

ensuite/puis	*then* ✓
suite à cela	*following that* ✓
finalement	*finally*
tout d'abord	*first of all* ✓
en ce moment/actuellement	*at the moment, currently*
toutes les semaines/tous les jours	*every week/every day*
une fois par mois	*once a month*
souvent/régulièrement	*often/regularly* ✓
de temps en temps	*from time to time*
pendant les vacances	*during the holidays*
rarement	*rarely*

Expressing likes and dislikes

J'aime bien/J'aime surtout ...	*I like/I like above all ...*
Je m'intéresse à ...	*I'm interested in ...*
J'ai horreur de ...	*I loathe ...*

Expressing opinions

Je pense que/Je trouve que/Je crois que ...	*I think that ...*
Je suis d'avis que ...	*I'm of the opinion that ...* ✓
Je suis (tout à fait) d'accord	*I (completely) agree* ✓
Je suis (totalement) pour ...	*I'm (totally) in favour of ...* ✓
Je suis absolument contre ...	*I'm completely against ...* ✓

Numbers and statistics

la moitié (de)/plus de la moitié (de)	*half (of)/more than half (of)*
un tiers (de)	*a third (of)*
un quart (de)	*a quarter (of)*
environ	*about* ✓
presque	*nearly*
un sur dix	*one in ten*
trois virgule cinq	*three point five*
en moyenne	*on average*
selon un sondage récent/une enquête récente	*according to a recent survey* ✓
selon les statistiques	*according to statistics*
il semble que	*it seems that*
il est évident que	*it's obvious that*
en plus	*in addition, what's more*
par contre	*on the other hand* ✓

Talking about the future

Ce week-end, je fais ...	*This weekend, I'm doing ...*
Je vais + infinitif	*I'm going to ...*
Je voudrais/J'aimerais + infinitif	*I'd like to ...*
J'ai envie de + infinitif	*I'd like to ...*
J'espère + infinitif	*I hope to ...*
Je compte/Je pense + infinitif	*I'm thinking of ...*
J'ai l'intention de/J'envisage de + infinitif	*I'm intending to ...*

Expressing rights and duties

Je peux + infinitif	*I can ...*
J'ai le droit de + infinitif	*I'm allowed to ...*
On me permet de + infinitif	*I'm allowed to ...*
On ne me permet pas de + infinitif	*I'm not allowed to ...*
Je dois + infinitif	*I have to ...*
Je suis obligé(e) de + infinitif	*I have to ...*

Impersonal verbs

Il faut + infinitif	*You have to, you must ...*
Il ne faut pas + infinitif	*You don't have to, you mustn't ...*
Il s'agit de + noun or infinitif	*It's a question of ...*
Il vaut mieux + infinitif	*It's better to ...*
Il convient de + infinitif	*It's appropriate to ...*

Giving advice

Moi, je + conditionnel	*I'd ...*
Tu pourrais + infinitif	*You could ...*
Tu devrais + infinitif	*You ought to ...*
Si j'étais toi/vous, je + conditionnel	*If I were you, I'd ...*
À ta/votre place, je + conditionnel	*If I were you, I'd ...*
Pourquoi est-ce que tu ne ...?	*Why don't you ... ?*
As-tu déjà essayé de + infinitif	*Have you tried ... ?*

Should have

J'aurais dû + infinitive	*I should have ...*
J'aurais pu + infinitive	*I could have ...*

Stating your argument

Moi, je trouve que ...	*I think that ...*
Pour moi, il est important de ...	*For me, it's important to ...*
Je suis convaincu(e) que ...	*I'm convinced that ...*
Je crois personnellement que ...	*Personally, I think that ...*
Je ne suis pas du tout d'accord parce que ...	*I really don't agree that ...*
Au contraire, moi je pense que ...	*On the contrary, I think that ...*
En revanche, je crois plutôt que ...	*On the other hand, I think that ...*
Oui, mais il ne faut pas oublier que ...	*Yes, but you mustn't forget that ...*

Phrases which take the subjunctive

il n'est pas sûr que/ce n'est pas certain que	*it's not certain that*
il est essentiel que	*it's essential that*
il est nécessaire que/il faut que	*it's necessary that*
il est possible que	*it's possible that*
avoir peur que	*to fear that*
vouloir/ne pas vouloir que	*to want/not to want that*
refuser que	*to refuse that*
c'est dommage que	*it's a pity that*
exiger que	*to demand that*

Topic vocabulary

Unit 1 En famille et entre amis

en famille/entre amis	*in the family/among friends*
une famille nombreuse/monoparentale	*large/single parent family*
des parents célibataires	*single parents*
une fête de famille	*a family celebration*
(provoquer) une dispute	*(to cause) an argument*
se disputer avec	*to argue with*
se calmer	*to calm down*
faire des choses ensemble	*to do things together*
exigeant	*demanding*
respecter les goûts de quelqu'un	*to respect someone's tastes*
s'entendre (bien) avec	*to get on well with*
avoir de bonnes relations avec	*to have a good relationship with*
rester en contact avec	*to stay in contact with*
rompre avec	*to break up with*
résoudre des conflits/un problème	*to resolve conflicts/a problem*
éviter le conflit	*to avoid conflict*
savoir écouter	*to be a good listener*
être là pour quelqu'un	*to be there for someone*
le mariage/se marier avec	*marriage/to marry*
le divorce/divorcer/se séparer	*divorce/to divorce/to separate*
le déclin du mariage	*the decline of marriage*
le taux de divorce/de naissance	*the divorce/birth rate*
vivre en concubinage/vivre avec	*to live with (someone)*
être un bon père/une bonne mère	*to be a good father/mother*
la maltraitance	*ill-treatment/abuse*
(rester) célibataire	*(to stay) single*
un(e) partenaire (pour la vie)	*a partner (for life)*
(tenir) une promesse	*(to keep) a promise*
fidèle/la fidélité	*faithful/faithfulness*

Unit 2 En pleine forme?

boire un coup	*to have a drink*
la consommation d'alcool	*alcohol consumption*
le tabagisme	*smoking*
provoquer (un cancer)	*to cause (cancer)*
prendre le volant	*to drive/get behind the wheel*
les drogues licites/ilicites/dures	*legal/illegal/hard drugs*
nuisible/nuire à	*damaging/to damage*
les médicaments	*medicine(s)*
se droguer/utiliser	*to take drugs/to use*
se mettre à (la cocaïne)	*to start taking (cocaine)*
une dose/surdose (ou overdose)	*a dose/overdose*
dépendant de/entraîner une dépendance	*addicted to/to cause an addiction*
être accro à	*addicted to*
un centre de désintoxication	*a detox centre*
manger équilibré	*to eat a balanced diet*
grignoter	*to snack, nibble*
nourrissant	*nourishing*
opter pour	*to opt for*
limiter/éviter/se priver de	*to limit/avoid/go without*
un plat cuisiné	*a ready meal*
une recette simple/rapide/saine	*a simple/quick/healthy recipe*
plein de (sel/matières grasses)	*full of (salt/fat)*
des troubles alimentaires	*eating disorders*
l'anorexie/la boulimie	*anorexia/bulimia*
prendre plaisir aux repas	*to enjoy meals*
prendre/perdre du poids	*to gain/lose weight*
obèse/l'obésité	*obese/obesity*
mener une vie équilibrée	*to lead a balanced life*
prendre du temps pour soi	*to take time for oneself*
consulter un médecin	*to consult a doctor*
l'espérance de vie	*life expectancy*
prendre ses propres décisions	*to make your own decisions*

Unit 3 Les médias

le lecteur/l'auditeur/le spectateur	*the reader/listener/viewer*
le feuilleton/le journal télévisé	*the soap/the TV news*
les informations/les actualités	*the news*
se tenir au courant	*to keep up (with current events)*
être bien informé(e)	*to be well informed*
l'émission/la chaîne	*the programme/the channel*
diffuser	*to broadcast*
la presse écrite/la presse gratuite	*the written press/the free press*

le quotidien/l'hebdomadaire/le mensuel	*the daily/weekly/monthly*
la télé-réalité	*reality TV*
le reportage/le documentaire	*the report/the documentary*
aborder un sujet important	*to tackle an important subject*
une bonne/mauvaise influence	*a good/bad influence*
l'inactivité/la passivité	*inactivity/passivity*
la publicité	*advertising*
le message caché	*the hidden message*
le sondage	*the survey*
la concurrence	*the competition*
renforcer des stéréotypes	*to reinforce stereotypes*
donner de bons conseils	*to give good advice*

Unit 4
Les nouveaux médias et la musique

utiliser/un utilisateur	*a user*
le chat/chatter	*chat/to chat (online)*
télécharger/le téléchargement	*to download/a download*
la messagerie instantanée	*instant messaging*
le logiciel	*software*
le lecteur MP3	*an MP3 player*
un ordinateur portable	*a laptop*
un casque audio	*headphones*
une clé USB	*a USB stick*
un appareil-photo numérique	*a digital camera*
partager des fichiers	*to share files*
bloguer/un blogueur	*to blog/a blogger*
s'exprimer (sans tabous)	*to express oneself (freely)*
en ligne	*online*
un internaute/l'internet	*an internet user/the internet*
fiable/la fiabilité	*reliable/reliability*
l'accès sans fil	*wireless access*
éteindre	*to switch off*
joindre quelqu'un	*to get in touch with someone*
un abonné/un abonnement	*a subscriber/a subscription*
un SMS/envoyer un SMS	*a text/to send a text*
naviguer sur le Web/la Toile/le Net	*to surf the web*
la messagerie électronique	*e-mail*
un moteur de recherche	*a search engine*
le consommateur	*the consumer*
s'informer sur	*to find out about*
commander (au cybermarché)	*to order (on the web)*
le risque de vol/de fraude	*the risk of theft/fraud*

inciter à la violence/au racisme	*to incite violence/racism*
être connecté	*to be connected (to the internet)*

Unit 5 La culture des loisirs

un acteur/une actrice	*actor/actress*
un rédacteur/une rédactrice	*editor*
un(e) cinéaste	*film-maker*
un auteur	*author*
un chanteur/une chanteuse	*singer*
un musicien/une musicienne	*musician*
un compositeur	*composer*
un artiste-peintre/sculpteur	*painter/sculptor*
un écrivain	*author*
un dramaturge	*playwright*
une œuvre	*a work (of art)*
un genre	*a type (of art)*
tourner/réaliser un film	*to make a film*
une animation	*a cartoon*
en noir et blanc/en couleur	*in black and white/in colour*
les effets spéciaux	*the special effects*
un film à gros budget	*a big budget film*
les sous-titres/doublé	*subtitles/dubbed*
le critique/la critique	*critic/film review*
une séance	*a showing/screening*
un cinéphile	*a film fan*
la Nouvelle Vague	*the new wave*
aborder des problèmes (sociaux)	*to tackle (social) problems*
connaître un succès fou	*to be very successful*
la télévision à écran large/plat	*wide/flat screen tv*
la scène/le metteur en scène	*the stage/the director*
un mime	*mime artist*
un saltimbanque	*acrobat*
un bateleur/jongleur	*juggler*
un prestidigitateur	*conjuror*

Unit 6 Vivre sa vie

le logement	*housing*
loger	*to live/stay*
sans domicile	*homeless*
le loyer	*rent*
HLM (habitation à loyer modéré)	*council housing*
(payer) une caution	*to pay a deposit*
s'installer en couple	*to set up home as a couple*
le foyer des jeunes	*hostel for young people*
le consommateur	*consumer*

la société de consommation	consumer society
faire des achats en ligne	to shop online
le cybershopping	online shopping
le shopping responsable	responsible shopping
la commerce équitable	fair trade
la mode éthique	ethical fashion
acheter à credit	to buy on credit
une dette	a debt
s'endetter/faire des dettes	to get into debt
conduire	to drive
le permis de conduire	driving licence
les transports en commun	public transport
un accident de la route	a road accident
un parc-relais	a park and ride scheme
un embouteillage	a traffic jam
embouteillé	congested
travailler à domicile/chez soi	to work from home
travailler à son rythme	to work at one's own pace
fonder une enterprise	to start a business
embaucher du personnel	freedom of expression
des missions de volontariat	voluntary projects
la parenthèse utile	gap year

Unit 7 Allez les sportifs

le parapente	hang gliding
le saut à l'élastique	bungee jumping
l'escrime	fencing
le tir	shooting
le sport individuel/d'équipe	individual/team sport
pratiquer un sport	to do a sport
se maintenir en forme	to keep fit
garder la ligne	to keep your figure
éviter le stress	to avoid stress
retrouver la forme après une maladie	to get fit after an illness
s'entraîner (pour un marathon)	to train (for a marathon)
la décontraction	relaxation
un débutant/un joueur experimenté	a beginner/inexperienced player
mener une vie sédentaire/active	to lead a sedentary/active life
un manque d'activité	a lack of activity
un bon état de santé	a good state of health
les risques de l'inactivité	the risks of inactivity
les os/les poumons/les artères	bones/lungs/arteries
les bienfaits du sport (sur le plan physique/mental)	the benefits of health (on a physical/mental level)

respirer	*to breathe*
lutter contre le surpoids	*to battle against overweight*
développer l'esprit d'équipe	*to develop team spirit*
la confiance en soi	*self confidence*
une médaille d'or	*a gold medal*
la blessure	*injury*
gagner/remporter/décrocher une médaille	*to win a medal*
les championnats du monde	*world championships*
gagner/perdre	*to win/to lose*
tricher/se disputer	*to cheat/to argue*
la victoire/la défaite	*victory/defeat*
gagner le respect des autres	*to be respected by others*
l'adversaire/le co-équipier	*opponent/team-mate*
l'arbitre/les officiels/les spectateurs	*the referee/the officials/the spectators*
montrer du respect envers quelqu'un	*to have respect for someone*
le dopage	*drug-taking (in sport)*
le comportement	*behaviour*
rejeter la violence/le racisme	*to reject violence/racism*

Unit 8 Le tourisme

les grandes vacances/les vacances d'hiver	*summer/winter holidays*
le vacancier/la vacancière	*holidaymaker*
le retour à la nature	*return to nature*
faire une croisière	*to do a cruise*
l'accent sur le luxe	*an accent on luxury*
le camping sauvage	*camping (in a field)*
à la recherche de ...	*in search of ...*
l'hébergement	*accommodation*
bronzer	*to sunbathe*
s'allonger sur la plage	*to lie on the beach*
attraper un coup de soleil	*to get sunstroke*
une ambiance décontractée	*a relaxed atmosphere*
éviter le (moindre) stress	*to avoid (any) stress*
découvrir (une région)	*to discover (a region)*
faire une randonnée (en montagne)	*to walk (in the mountains)*
faire la grasse matinée	*to have a lie-in*
l'écotourisme	*ecotourism*
respecter l'environnement	*to respect the environment*
se rapprocher de la nature	*to get close to nature*
contribuer à l'économie locale	*to contribute to the local economy*
limiter/trier ses déchets	*to limit/separate rubbish*
économiser l'eau/l'energie	*to economise on water/energy*

limiter son impact sur l'environnement	*to limit one's impact on the environment*
un nombre préoccupant de visiteurs	*a worrying number of visitors*
un climat agréable	*a pleasant climate*
la circulation routière	*traffic*
un embouteillage/un bouchon	*a traffic jam*
la paralysie des centre-villes	*the paralysis of town centres*
les accidents de la route (mortels)	*(fatal) road accidents*

Unit 9 Le lycée et après

passer un examen	*to take an exam*
réussir/être reçu(e) à un examen	*to pass an exam*
le taux de réussite (du bac)	*the pass rate (of the 'bac')*
les conseils d'orientation	*careers advice*
l'école maternelle	*nursery school*
une épreuve (obligatoire)	*a (compulsory) test*
le système éducatif	*the education system*
en seconde	*in Year 11*
en première	*in the AS/Lower 6th year*
en terminale	*in the A2/Upper 6th year*
stressant/stressé	*stressful/stressed*
le stress/l'angoisse	*stress*
motivant	*motivating*
redoubler (une année scolaire)	*to retake (a school year)*
un programme chargé	*a heavy timetable*
à la fac	*at university*
le soutien/manque de soutien	*support/lack of support*
l'incertitude de l'avenir	*uncertainty about the future*
un contrôle	*a test*
faire un apprentissage	*to do an apprenticeship*
décrocher/trouver un emploi	*to get a job*
être au chômage	*to be unemployed*
la formation professionnelle	*professional training*
le taux de chômage	*the unemployment rate*
la vie active	*working life*
le manque d'expérience	*lack of experience*
la formation en alternance	*sandwich training*
bien rémunéré	*well paid*
une position permanente/à plein temps	*a permanent/full time job*
un emploi temporaire	*a temporary job*
l'autonomie financière	*financial independence*
le RMI (revenu minimal d'insertion)	*the minimum wage*
un contrat à durée déterminée	*a fixed-term contract*
une lettre de motivation	*an application letter*

Page 15
a) B   **b)** B   **c)** A

Page 16
(1) indépendant   **(2)** bonnes   **(3)** meilleur   **(4)** devenir   **(5)** droit
(6) refusent   **(7)** liberté

Page 17
Vicky **C**   Adèle **H**   Samuel **D**   Charles **A**   Jules **G**

Page 18
(a) to appear grown-up/to keep in contact with friends at all times.
(b) because of the health risks/because they are expensive and children
might lose them. **(c)** a child who goes out alone can ring the parents if there
is a problem/s/he will use the house telephone much less, which is useful if
parents want to use it themselves or are expecting an important call.

Page 20
1 Thibaut, Jean   **2** Camille   **3** Saïda   **4** -   **5** Thibaut, Jean, Camille

Page 21
a Ils consomment des boissons gazeuses.
b Ils favorisent la perte de calcium dans l'urine.
c Ils boivent moins de lait et ils ne font pas assez d'activité physique

Grammar

(1) alcoolisme (m.), obésité (f.), niveau (m.), tolérance (f.), mariage (m.),
certitude (f.). journaux, portables, prix (-), émissions, conflits.

(2) ce travail, ces candidats, de l'effort, du tourisme, toutes les idées.

(3) une émission intéressante, de bonnes idées, un livre fascinant, de la
mauvaise publicité, une jeune actrice ambitieuse.

(4) mon sport préféré, ses baskets, notre équipe, ton but, leur victoire.

(5) elle comprend facilement; il est le meilleur footballeur; est-ce qu'elle
parle aussi vite normalement? est-ce que les garçons sont plus sportifs
que les filles?

(6) Tu habites à quelle distance de Nantes? Les vêtements sont-ils en
bonne condition? Il travaille à la banque depuis deux ans. Vous lui avez
parlé de son avenir? J'ai passé la soirée chez Marion.

(7) Tu le vois? Est-ce qu'elle lui écrira? Ils y vont sans nous? Nous ne
nous amusons pas.

(8) Your own answer.

9 Elle nous téléphone chaque soir. Ils lui écrivent toutes les semaines. Je le lui ai déjà dit. Nous vous le donnerons. Tu peux me le répéter?

10 C'est celui dont la femme est directrice? C'est le stylo que tu cherches? Avec qui allez-vous en vacances? C'est un film que j'ai beaucoup apprécié. Je lui ai montré le bureau où je travaille.

11 Quelle robe préfères-tu? Celle avec la ceinture? Il aime bien mon ordinateur, mais il a des difficultés avec le sien. Vos idées ne sont pas mauvaises, mais les nôtres sont meilleures! Lequel des deux? Celui aux cheveux blonds?

12 Il déteste réviser. Après avoir fini, je suis parti. Tu veux partir maintenant? Après être arrivés, ils nous ont téléphoné.

13 Tu viens? Ils prennent. Nous allons. Il finit. Elles attendent. Je peux. Elle voit. Vous écrivez.

14 j'ai fait, ils ont pris, nous sommes allés, elle s'est lavée, tu as mis, il a parlé, vous êtes rentrés, elles ont bu

15 je lisais, tu finissais, elle buvait, nous travaillions, vous alliez, ils faisaient

16 Your own answer.

17 je devrai, tu vendras, il se levera, nous saurons, vous verrez, ils choisiront

18 Qu'est-ce que tu vas faire ce soir? Tu penses à aller au théâtre? Tu iras encore en vacances? Quand tu auras vingt ans tu seras à l'université. Auras-tu reçu la lettre?

19 Your own answer.

20 Your own answer.

21 Je ne suis pas sûr que ce soit réaliste. Elle voudrait que j'arrive à l'heure. Pour arriver ce soir, il faut que vous partiez tout de suite.

22 Ce sera fait. Cela n'a pas été fini. La lettre n'a pas été écrite.

23 Your own answer.